Musical Birds of Nevada

Silence! Meadowlark Singing

George Griffith

Photographs by Alan Gubanich, Doug Ramseth, Bill Bolton
Cartoons by Charlie Kahn

iUniverse, Inc.
New York   Bloomington

Musical Birds of Nevada
Silence! Meadowlark Singing

iUniverse books may be ordered through booksellers or by contacting:

iUniverse
1663 Liberty Drive
Bloomington, IN 47403
www.iuniverse.com
1-800-Authors (1-800-288-4677)

ISBN: 978-1-4401-1508-0 (pbk)
ISBN: 978-1-4401-1509-7 (ebk)

Library of Congress Control Number: 2009922452

Printed in the United States of America

iUniverse rev. date: 2/5/2009

Contents

Acknowledgments and Credits

Thanks must first go to my wife, Suzanne Griffith (a misplaced Sandwich Islander-not a Kanaka, but a local kama'aina full of the spirit of aloha), motivated, not by the mythical menehunes, but perhaps by her mother BYRD Lacy.

Dr.Alan Gubanich, Vice President of Lahontan Audubon Society, Professor Emeritus Ornithology, has distinguished himself as an avian photographer. He has provided many of the individual photographs, excepting the American Robin, first Blackbird, Western Sandpiper provided by Doug Ramseth, the Condor captured by Bill Bolton and the Scrub-jay.

Charlie Kahn, a Down-Easterner from Kennebunk, Maine, and world famous but still largely unknown plastic sculptor, has drawn on a 45-year pastime of creating cartoons to amplify the lighthearted approach for this work.

This less-than-serious tone was suggested by musician John Roos who recognized the virtues of the combined subject of music, birds, and Nevada. I am also indebted to two individuals whom I will mention allegorically. The first is the intrepid little lady personified with the name Myrtle Entwhistle(not her real name) who gave the first outcry of disapproval. She is to be thanked for her contributions, advice, and her deep knowledge of the subject. Grateful acknowledgement is also given to the name Tall Major-General Henry Gastille Franklinheim, who is bald as a coot and crazy as a jaybird. Along with bird stories, his contributions include boring recollections of his early years, military service, and historical stories of the Boer

War, particularly the Relief of Ladysmith; he loves to retell them but none are included here. Cordial thanks go also to the Baron Ludwig von Henhousen. He is characterized by his slogan "ILLEGITIMUS NON-TATUM CARBORUNDUM"; he lives in Cambria(and Harmony), California. Thanks to Kevin Griffith, of Irvine, California, who has twice read and made critiques of the Ms.

Their editing and keen eyes for errors (providing early marking in the marginalia) are appreciated.

Gratitude is offered to a Mainer, a relentless young bird(in his 80s) John La Flamme, a frequent visitor to Nevada, who survived a gondola accident in the French Alps, and who also made it over Donner Pass in an October snowstorm using a bottle of GammelDansk as fuel. I am grateful to Libbie Shimer who has critiqued the galley proofs and used her artistic talents to provide the painting shown on the front cover(Western Meadowlark). The suggestions of Bruce Pruitt are appreciated. Thanks to leaders(of great expertise) on Lahontan Audubon birding trips and others who wish to remain completely anonymous; I have refrained from adding the names of other friends whose stimulation and largesse of ideas have been invaluable. Direct and helpful quotes and references are noted and are especially appreciated.

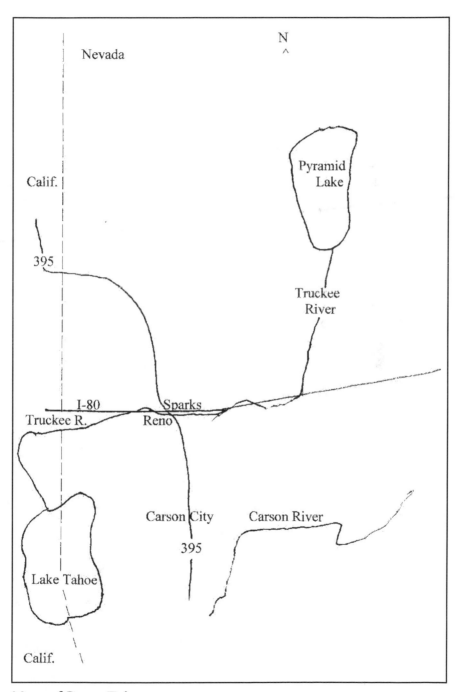

Map of Reno-Tahoe area

Overture

*"Where I live-there are rainbows, with flowers full of color,
and birds filled with song"*

from the song *Hawaiian Lullaby*
by Peter Moon and Hector Venegas

Almost everyone living in Nevada develops affection for birds, wild horses, bears, marmots and certain other wildlife. Nevada has a most diverse bird environment: alpine meadows, rich farmland, valley wetlands, lofty mountains with coniferous forests, foothills covered with pines, manzanita, scrub and other chaparral brush and shrubs populated with small birds, low and high desert-land covered with sagebrush, lakes and urban locales all presenting a potpourri of birds' music.

The region discussed, rich with bird migration and also a home for many bird species, is the narrow geographical area of northern Nevada, and even more precisely the Reno-Tahoe area near the Pacific Fly-way and the In-land Fly-way. For a small city, Reno has an unusually large number of parks filled with bird songs. Summer residents migrate to warmer places in the fall and return in April and May.

Adding to the bird population is also the North-south Intermountain Fly-way touching eastern Nevada. Most birds travel over land where there are thermals, although some large birds rely on ocean wind currents to rise and float, changing directions, actions not unlike principles of sailing.

This book is about musical birds, both native and migratory. Authors, composers and poets (Coleridge,

Whitman, Longfellow, Thoreau, Keats, Beethoven, Messiaen, Vivaldi, Mozart, Old Testament prophets, to name a few) have extolled the beauty of bird's singing. While there are many lists and descriptions of birds and also other sources that define and elaborate on the subject of music, this combines the subjects of birds and music related to the environs of Nevada.

The aim here is not merely to describe birds but to depict the nature of bird-singing and their singing mechanism with focus on the enjoyment of bird music, interesting characteristics of song-birds, and music itself. This brief treatise is a scattering of material specifically describing song-birds(oscines) of Nevada and how they sing, covering a limited number of bird species ranging from the Yellow-rumped Warbler to a variety of snow-birds (no jail-birds) and other birds that are just passing through this area, using the fly-ways.

Until a few decades ago, the generation of music by birds has defied understanding. This book was written in a patio-home in Reno, with interruptions from activities of jays, finches, doves and flickers on a simple bird-feeder hanging on the deck. It is an attempt to make the understanding of birds and bird-singing available to a wide spectrum of readers including young adults who want to broaden their knowledge of birds, bird music, related physics, ornithology, biology and music itself. Perhaps it will contribute to those with a birding background. The area has a rich nature of the American West that attracted Europeans, especially the Basques, early settlers of the area.

Even though it seems that many birds are not musical, birds have encouraged the development of many early human musical styles, such as unresolved chords, the canon and the solo song. For example, the Mourning Dove provides one of the sweetest songs in the universe.

With a discussion of vocal capabilities of birds and the corresponding human vocal functions, this writing is intended to inform, inspire, and bring a smile to the naturalist, music-lover, and light reader. At the same time, it is both a brief scientific study and an attempt to help one unwind. It is a half-serious and half-lighthearted attempt to correlate and incorporate the latest research studies of birds and music and is peppered with a few facts and factoids here and there and, without a doubt, it may contain a kernel of truth.

This discussion has been aided by research carried out by many others. The Cornell Lab of Ornithology has provided, on the internet, a ready source of bird-songs for listening. They have also made available an audio booklet featuring songs of 250 birds, a further encouragement for this writing, and for good listening; this audio booklet can also be a good tool, on the porch or deck, for attracting birds.

Many studies have been carried out in laboratories, such as one at the University of Western Ontario, and by researchers such as Dr. Scott A. Macdougall-Shackelton, who must occupy an exceptional place in research studies. The Lahontan Audubon Society of Reno provides many opportunities for those wishing to expand their birding knowledge and experiences in this locale.

Do not let it ruffle your feathers or drive you cuckoo, but poetic license has been taken in this experimental work; it is not an exhaustive study in itself, hardly even(pardon the pun)a bird's-eye view. Partly for that reason, the second volume is already in the planning stage. The second volume, in large print for ageing eyes, will be "Musical Birds of Nevada for the Elderly" describing an even more limited number of birds and their music. The reality is that as some people grow older, their hearing reception and frequency response becomes narrow, sometimes reduced from 15,000 Hertz to a range of 250 to 1500 hertz, making it nearly impossible to receive songs from many birds. This last volume will be appropriate for our citizenry who leave home in mid-afternoon for "early-bird" specials. There are birders and there are early-birders.

It is my hope that this book will stimulate and advance the art of listening, the subject of the penultimate chapter.

Numerous footnotes would be confusing, so we close with a section called "Bibliography", a source of some highlighted quotations, information and further reading. It is a mere fraction of available bird literature.

The melodies of these exuberant songsters never grow old. Realizing that the early bird gets the worm, this book may speak to you about the nature of bird music while advancing interest in song-birds and the evolution of music; or it may just be a relaxing Sunday afternoon browse.

The question is this: what is bird music? We will step behind the scenes and let it happen. This is the real macaw.

European Starling

"Today's Kids----"

Northern Mockingbird

Song Sparrow

Summary Daybreak

"When thro' the woods and forest glades I wander, And hear the birds sing sweetly in the trees."

from the hymn *How Great Thou Art*

Birds announce daybreak. Although summer extends from the end of spring until the beginning of autumn, we begin by focusing attention on the advent of summer. This is the period, not that others are exempt, when the yellow-headed (and Brewer's) blackbirds and robins make themselves known. Two mockingbirds with complex songs are becoming friendly in Bartley Park in Reno. Little birds are sitting on the railings and budding tree limbs making a celestial concert. The Truckee is flowing rapidly and the river brush is filled with birds with song. Serenades of Nevada birds can be heard mostly in early spring through late autumn. However, doves, finches, Northern flickers and Steller's jays among others, have spent the winter here.

Vogelgesang is the German word for "birds singing". Songs of birds are such early and basic forms of music that a stop on some pipe organs has even been labeled "Vogelgesang". A corresponding organ stop in English is called "nightingale". Musical instruments copy bird-singing. Composers, such as Handel in his *Cuckoo and the Nightingale* (Concerto for the Organ), have copied bird songs. Mozart considered the songs of a bird to be every bit as musical as that of a human.

Summer is the time of the year when most songbirds appear. Ethereal arias of these arrivistes brighten our world. Daybreak is usually the time of day when the music of birds is at its best, awakening us from our slumber. It is rumored that Albert Einstein once pointed out that "The problem with the speed of light is that it comes too early in the morning".

As someone pointed out, one swallow does not make a summer; but friends, take a gander.

Mourning Dove

American Robin

California Quail

"Not every candidate has ---"

How Birds Sing and Communicate

Down in the forest something stirred
It was only the note of a bird.

"Down in the Forest" by Harold Simpson

Two often-used classifications of birds are perching (or passerine) and non-passerine, such as the bobwhite quail and western meadowlarks that nest on the ground. Birds of both classifications sing. Most believe that birds sing to announce territory, to attract mates, to respond to threats and for enjoyment.

Birds have no conservatory and therefore they cannot read music; however, they, mostly males, can sing and some have the gift of relative pitch. Birds not only make music, but they respond to music; some copy other birds' songs. To describe the music of birds in some words is not an easy task. Birds sing beautiful melodies, but they do not use a regular metric time, except for trills, and they usually leave a phrase unresolved. Some bird music seems joyful; other music has a sad characteristic. Both birds and human beings take pleasure in music and they may respond to one another.

While the conversation of people is usually in the range between about 870 Hertz(bass) and 1200Hertz(soprano) plus overtones, birds tend to vocalize up to 4200Hertz(Hz), the top of the piccolo range, with some going much higher in frequency. Song-birds are musical instruments. Sounds are produced by modulation of air causing sound-waves. Birds sing and hear at a higher range than the average human frequency response. We often identify bird music by our knowledge of solfege, and it is important to realize that there are only twelve musical notes, or multiples thereof, from "A" through "G#" whether sung by a human or a bird. The musical pitch of the note "A" is generally considered to be 440 Hertz or some even multiple. Frequencies of 880,1320 and even 220 Hertz are considered "A". Some birds' songs even suggest a key; the Common Loon may be singing the key of G.

Bird songs are generated by air vibrations that are modified in a way very unique to the species. Birds produce sounds or sound waves that, like all sound waves, involve frequency generation through various means: vibration or changes in pressure, stress, particle displacement or particle velocity propagated in an elastic material.

Examples are wind through tuned organ pipes, vibrating violin strings, and human vocal chords. Therefore the physical laws of organ pipes describe one aspect of bird song generation.

Sound waves can be defined by a complex formula involving time, propagation speed, pressure, and the three coordinates(x,y,z) of space.

For an open pipe or other air column of length L where V is the velocity of sound in air, the frequencies(F) of vibration for the fundamental and the first three overtones are

$$F_0 = V/2L$$
$$F_1 = 2V/2L$$
$$F_2 = 3V/2L$$
$$F_3 = 4V/2L$$

Those formulas are the physics of frequency generation in open pipes or columns of air.

"All singing birds are much pleased with (music), especially nightingales—"

Robert Burton's *The Anatomy of Melancholy*,
year 1621

Sound waves are also the received sensations produced in the ear of the human being(or bird). After birds set air into motion, into vibrations, it is modified on the way to the beak, producing a variety of distinctive sounds. Birds set air in motion in a unique system somewhat different from the human instrument. Both human beings and birds have a trachea, or windpipe, that funnels the air to the bronchi, the two main branches.

Instead of the human larynx, birds have a syrinx, which varies in size from one species to the other. The syrinx may be an alternate name for the Pandian Pipes, an instrument of antiquity.

The organ called the syrinx is located where the trachea meets the bronchial tubes. From air sacs, air is projected through lungs into the syrinx. The syrinx is a song-box containing a thin membrane called the tympaniformis interna. Internal labia(or lips) act on the moving air and, together with the syrinx, produce the unique sounds.

Sound generation involves vibration of the two-dimensional membrane or membranes and oscillations in the three-dimensional space in the syrinx and other parts of the system. Different songs result from different resonant patterns of vibrating air in the sryinx and the various waveguides or pipes leading to the beak. Bird-songs are developed in an instrument just as unique but seemingly more complex than a pipe organ or even a violin.

In summary, bird songs, like all sound waves, are oscillations which originate and travel through waveguides, which are the syrinx and trachea. In addition to the harmonics generated in these wave guides and other organs, the sound is further developed and more harmonics are generated as the sound passes through the throat and mouth (beak).

The sounds produced, like all sound, travel at the velocity of 1127 feet per second in dry air (of Nevada) at 20 degrees fahrenheit. The received pitches of songs of birds in flight will rise as the bird approaches and decrease as the bird flies away. Older people tend to experience losses of hearing at the higher end of the frequency spectrum and may not be able to hear certain birds.

After listening to bird songs and checking pitches with the help of a piano, it becomes apparent that most birds sing in the treble clef, and above middle C, the note on the line below the staff, or the C near the middle on the piano. Many perching birds sing in the range up to 4 kilohertz and above.

Birds provide melodies, symphonies and fugues, among other styles, but these songs are seldom resolved to the key-tone or fundamental (tonic), unlike most human compositions. Bird-sound characteristics fall into two categories, mainly. They are 1)Plosives and 2) Fricatives, where plosives are described as first blocking the sound path and then opening it creating a puff of air. Fricatives result from blowing air through a narrow orifice such as in human whistling. Mourning doves have a sound more akin to a human nasal sound. Because of birds' singing mechanism being more similar to pipes or circular waveguide, the timbre of bird melodies can be more easily reproduced on a pipe organ, clarinet, flute, or piccolo than on a piano.

The California Gull demonstrates its ability to communicate. On Nevada Beach at Lake Tahoe, it turns it head upward and sliding up from an accidental, A Flat, it sings about eight A notes, saying, "Give me part of that sandwich that I see". An A- note(440 Hertz) also happens to be the pitch of a foghorn. It is the pitch or note most instruments tune to, led by the oboe in an orchestra. Birds often communicate with each other singing what is called "signal song".

Birds employ the musical concept of *ornamentals*, brief notes leading to the final pitch. Music composers have copied this technique.

Birds also make non-vocal sounds like 1) the drumming of a grouse by filling an extended esophagus, or 2) the percussion sound of flight of the quail or Mourning Dove. The mating and nesting season is the time when many birds sing.

Many authors have reasoned that the birds' vocal instruments have been created, harmonized and adjusted to praise God.

Bewick's Wren

Music and Bird Trivia

*"Do not revile the king even in your thoughts,
or curse the rich in your bedroom, because a bird of the air
may carry your words, and a bird on the wing may report
what you say"*

Ecclesiastes 10:20

*"Like a bird that strays from its nest,
is a man who strays from his home".*

Proverbs 27:8

Birds are to be respected and can set examples both good and bad for all mankind. Note those wise cautions.

If the birds in this volume bear any resemblance to or exhibit any traits of the reader, they may be only illusions. Unlike some authors, I will 1)endeavor to stick to the King's English, minimize tutelage, and avoid cliches, metaphors (especially mixed metaphors), fancy words, motto, allegories, hyperbole, double entendre, puns, redundant phrases, exaggeration, analogies, innuendo, political correctness, mumbo-jumbo, oxymorons, superficiality(only skin deep) and even mendacity and 2)make a last ditch effort to avoid banal detail. Those styles are not my cup of tea but I do not put all my eggs in one basket. I can hope that these camels do not get their noses under the tent. I may be going out on a limb, but from time to time, there may be attention to some minisculae and trivia.

There will now be an attempt to let the cat out of the bag regarding birds' songs and why birds sing. What is bird music? A little bird told me that Beethoven's First Symphony and Corelli's Concerto in G Major are not some of the early symphonic masterpieces. Many thousands of years ago, concerts were being performed in the forests and meadows. A few of these performers are identified and a different world of music will be presented in the spirit of days gone by. Some birds are wonderful singers.

The birds' songs are not conventional symphonies but are early forms of impressionistic music. Sometimes they seem to be messages from on high, as part of God's handiwork. Examples are the warbling of a Purple Finch or the piccolo tones of Western Meadow-larks or song sparrows. Their music interacts with the outside world with melancholy or bright tones, in a variety of moods, like other music. The song may end with a final dramatic statement(scherzo), juxtaposition, or arpeggio.

-And hear the pleasant cuckoo, loud and long.
The simple bird that thinks two notes a song.

By W.H.Davis,
from *Child Lovers: April's Charms*

A few birds, such as the Canada Goose, demonstrate the antithesis of good singing, especially while on the ground. These birds can be seen marching slowly, quietly, without concern, with a string of newborns across a busy street, such as Lakeside, near Virginia Lake in Reno, until a loud shriek is heard, a final song. Canada geese usually sing while in the air. They can be heard, as they become airborne, attacking with a high-C to F-sharp, a rather dissonant phrase called a tritone, an unpleasant pitch often included in a police, train or fire siren.

The dove's mournful song is a favorite. But rumor has it that one of our late presidents would go shooting doves near our nation's capitol, where a Mourning-dove met its untimely death. The opposing political party became ecstatic over this episode of malfeasance and kept it to announce as an October surprise. The chief's dove-hunting became an albatross around his neck (Thus we kill two birds with one stone).

What is the motivation for this book? It is no wild goose chase and there is no quid-pro-crow.

Someone recently commented on a particular jailbird, who, after being caught, sang like a canary. The canary is not the only singing bird. Nevada is full of chatterboxes like the Mountain and Steller's jays. The Nevada state-bird is the Mountain Bluebird, and a bird of more beauty can hardly be found.

In some instances, parts of the bird such as the wing, may provide a percussion-like sound. The wing is the bird's engine. All birds have two wings; humans proudly claim to be left-wing or right-wing, but not both. The bird's underbody is like a center-board or keel on a small boat. The tail is like a rudder on an airplane (or vice-versa). Both airplanes and music owe some design to birds. A skeleton of a bird's wing resembles that of a human arm. Some bones are hollow with internal webbing to lessen weight. Various other appendages are also significant. But it is unnecessary to have a degree in Aeronautical Engineering to understand birds.

The author, when it comes to naming birds while making notes in a hammock under two Jeffrey Pine trees in late summer, may be accused of being below the level of pigeon-english. However, drawing on a knowledge of music, he reveals his life entirely, nails his colors to the mast, puts the nose to the grindstone, paddles his own canoe, talks turkey, goes birding, checks hundreds of good references (the significant ones noted at the end), and pays the piper, to get this book underway. It is amazing to note that once this writing began, references pop up out of the nest everywhere. It is hoped that this effort is not a pig in the poke and that a dusty volume called "Musical Birds of Nevada" is not found years-hence pigeon-holed in a damp basement shelf or among the bats in the belfry.

Just a few different local birds, their music, and how they make music will be described. For example, how would one describe a duck? The first thing that comes to mind is that it is damp. Ducks'(and geese) squawks and honks are often similar to the sound of an engine being cranked by a low battery. Imagine the noise at the annual Great Truckee River Duck Race when more than 10,000 ducks are dumped into the Truckee River at Wingfield Park.

Birds' music is exciting in its variety, but it is not always satisfying. On more than one occasion, St. Francis of Assisi would stop and talk and even preach to birds thus quieting their chatter.

> *"Among the artistic hierarchy, birds are probably the greatest musicians to inhabit our earth"*
>
> by Olivier Messiaen

Messiaen composed *Abyss of the Birds* from *Quartet From the End of Time* and it was first played in a German prison camp during World War II.

Birds have songs and calls. An early motivation for the "Bo'sun's Call" in the Royal Navy, U.S.Navy and others, surely came from the awareness that a high-pitched bird-song instrument could be heard over the din of breaking wave, crying birds and running seas. The Bo'sun's Call is a small metal high-pitched pipe that is used for communications on navy ships to alert crews to various emergencies and events of the day. Of course, sound only exists as a sensation perceived by the ear, or as seen on an oscilloscope when the vibrations or sound waves reach the ear or instrument.

Most music, at least in the Western world, utilizes one of two modes, major and minor, or both. In major keys, solfege tones are usually separated by whole notes, except in two places in the major eight-note or diatonic scale, between the third and fourth, and between the seventh and eighth notes, where tones are separated by a half-interval or semi-tone. There are other tonal progressions. Prior to the diatonic scale, notes were set in basic modes, some of which could be related to songs of birds and perhaps early Arabic music. The pentatonic scale has five notes corresponding to the black keys on the piano. This is an early scale still in use in Japan and China.

Now, stringed instruments are tuned harmonically, starting with one pitch. An orchestra is often tuned by an A-note(usually based on 440 Hz) played on an oboe. The A-note has varied from 404 Hz in 1699 to 455 Hz in 1859. The pitch of 435 Hz was called the modern French pitch for the A-note. Pianos are tuned in an equal-tempered fashion with notes separated by a ratio, which is the square root of two, limiting perfect harmony to only the octaves. Early compositions by European composers were frequently written in a minor key and are especially beautiful. There are several different minor scales where the semitones are in different locations and not limited to two semitones.

Timbre is the color or makeup of the sound, a characterization of the amplitudes of the root pitch and the overtones. Timbre causes the listener to determine whether the instrument is a trumpet, violin, Mourning Dove or Crow.

Birds' songs sometimes seem to fall into a particular mode and its unique timbre. They include major, minor and dissonant intervals. Some have completely different modal arrangements and unique sequences providing ecstatic dimensions often pleasing to the human ear and reflecting God's creative power. When a bird song is described as starting on a major-third, it signifies the third note above the root or tonic of a major scale. A song resembling a *Picardy Third* (when a phrase sounding like a minor key concludes on a major key) has even been heard in thick Cottonwood and Aspen groves.

> *"And whenever the spirit from God troubled Saul, David took the harp and played; then Saul grew calm and he recovered, and the evil spirit left him".*
>
> I Samuel

At times we hear an arpeggio or framework of a familiar chord from birds. Many birds enjoy the ability to have relative pitch, copying other birds and sometimes instruments as well. Some songbirds can actually sing harmonious duets. Humans with absolute pitch can identify certain repeated keys or tone frequencies of mourning doves, for example.

We hear many styles. Some birds just sing. Some provide percussion, chatter, hoot, or screech. When quails, doves or grouse take flight, their wing noise is quite spectacular. The quality or characteristic of the tone of song birds is caused by a certain array of overtones (2nd, 3rd, 4$^{th \ and \ more}$ harmonics). As examples of such tones or timbre, violins and violas have large arrays of overtones or harmonics. Some birds have many harmonics and others very few resulting in a clear pitch in the style of an oboe, piccolo or whistle.

We hear *duets*; some birds have varied repertoire. Birds sing most often at daybreak. Nightingales sing at night, but also during the day. Although rarely heard, *polyphony* is a style probably copied or developed in Europe during the middle-ages, where melody and harmony coexist with harmony also being melodic. *Suspension* is where a note is held while other notes are moving. Some birds have the song pattern of *glissando* where the song drops or rises in pitch from the original note.

Ornaments appear frequently in bird songs and occasionally in human musical compositions. An ornament is short tone preceding the one targeted.

It is often a half-note or whole note higher or lower than the note of a longer time period to be sung.

Daniel J. Levitin, in his book *"This is Your Brain on Music"* states that music is organized sound. That being the case, many birds produce music, but as he further elaborates, "This organization may be something no one wants to listen to." Crows and (sometimes) gulls are examples of this. Their songs' main characteristics start with loudness. However, the cries of gulls can be a pleasant background sound and their flight patterns are a beauty to behold by one enjoying a stroll on the beach.

The following "Examples of Birds' Music" are samples of varieties of melodies heard from each example.

"You got to know---"

Bullock's Oriole

Western Meadowlark

Bob White Quail

Song Sparrow

California Quail

Common Loon

Examples of Birds' Songs

Examples of Birds' Songs

Early Birds, People, and Migration

"So God created the great creatures of the sea and every living and moving thing with which the water teems, according to their kinds, and every winged bird according to its kind. And God saw that it was good."

Genesis 1:21

It is believed that by intelligent design after the Big Bang was created some 14 billion years ago when the universe was formed from a primeval atom which started the expansion of the universe, Adam and Eve, and perhaps later the Australopithecus aferensis, and even later the Sumerians and the Semites and others of the Middle East and Africa, are the ancestors of early civilizations. Those civilizations developed in Persia and Babylon; perhaps other forerunners lived near the Olduvai Gorge of Africa. Other early civilizations include Arabs, Phoenicians, Celtics, and Native Americans. There is evidence of Native Americans in Nevada as early as 9,000 years ago. Descendants of these early humans are today's snow-birds (and jail-birds), often migratory species.

Long before (records of) these early people, dinosaurs roamed the earth, skeletons of huge birds have been found. During the last 100,000 years, these huge birds disappeared giving way to flamingos, herons, cranes, loons and the ibis in the wetlands, as well as eagles, falcons, gulls, and smaller songbirds nesting in the cottonwoods, willows, bulrushes, cattails, and marsh grasses and sagebrush of Nevada.

The earliest bird known from fossils, discovered in Germany over one-hundred years ago, is the *archaeopteryx(ar-kee-opt'-er-ix)* from the Jurassic period. Those fossil remains are in the Natural History Museum in England. Recently, researchers have found that later, in the early Cretaceous period some 120 million years ago, there existed the *orthocheirus* that could fly 500 kilometers with flaps of its 12-meter wings. Also in this period, another bird, the *tapejara,* used a bright red head-crest to attract mates. Smaller birds with head-crests do so today. Did those early birds go after worms? Probably not. Those large-bird groups, appearing after the Cambrian Explosion, are extinct.

The California Condor was a western native raptor prior to European settlements in this country. Almost extinct, they have been part of a captive breeding program and small numbers have been released into the wild. A large black bird, the California Condor flies hundreds of miles in search of food.

Most birds migrate. It is presumed that summer, with long periods of ultra-violet rays, may be necessary for breeding purposes. They have summer quarters and winter quarters (a few are bi-coastal). We have seen various jays return to the same nest year after year.

Swainson's Hawks breed in Nevada and other parts of the West, and migrate, because of our winter, to the Argentine Pampas, some 7,000 miles away. Annual retentive birds (that do not migrate), like those that migrate, commence courtship when summer approaches.

For a bird, unless wings are clipped, immigration is common and a state border is meaningless. Passports, visas, and green cards are unnecessary for our small avian friends. When birds migrate, they cannot see the borders. Arctic Terns travel nearly 12,000 miles (as the crow flies), from the Arctic to the Antarctic. Both global cooling and global warming have reliably been reported at Antarctica, usually with more ice melting each year. It is hoped that the terns will not be running on empty when they leave Antarctica. Also, due to the global warming cycle in the Northern Hemisphere, birds, such as the Roadrunner, Cactus Wren, and California quail from New Mexico, Arizona and Southern California are moving into Nevada. There is suspicion that their songs may be in Spanish. Dialects have actually been observed in birds' songs.

Birds of passage migrate in many paths, but in the United States there are four worthy of attention. Birds migrate along the coasts and along the Mississippi. Also in the west there is a path that resolves itself along the San Pedro River and the cottonwoods through Arizona into Mexico. The fly-ways through Nevada are significant. During daytime migration, birds have many ports of call in which to refresh themselves in food and water. A few species travel long distances non-stop. Some music birds, such as the Northern Bob White quail, do not migrate.

How birds migrate, often traveling hundreds or thousands of miles (as the Arctic Tern), has been a subject of mystery and wonder for ages. Many return to the same small area year after year. Most agree that birds use eyesight and familiar landmarks such as mountain ranges and river valleys. They may rely on earth's magnetism, heat seeking senses, and characteristics of earth's rotation. Other aspects of celestial navigation, especially at night, provide the most likely tools (before Global Positioning Systems), with focus on the moon and stars(variable stars are not useful), spatial relationships of sun and moon(in alignment or in quadrature), air currents and wind patterns all supported voyages of Henry the Navigator and other early ocean sailors.

Let us conclude that birds have their own unique and mysterious migrating system that we could call BPS, Bird Positioning Systems, involving an innate tendency and perhaps even an internal clock.

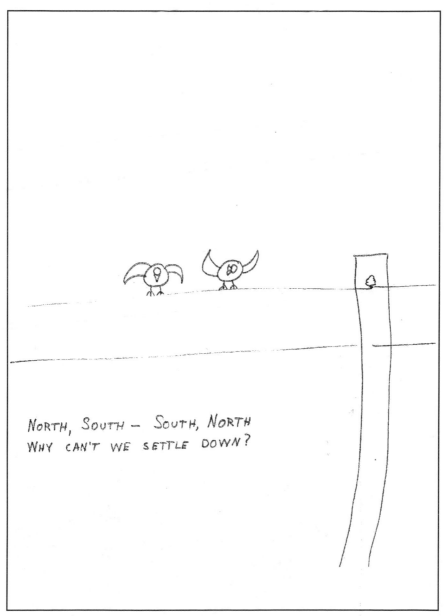

"North South-South North---"

Northern Flicker

Kildeer (doing a broken wing act)

Western Scrub Jay at Bird Feeder

Intermezzo

People can be like birds. Victor Hugo penned these thoughts:

"Let us be like the bird for a moment perched on a frail branch while he sings; though he feels it bend, yet he sings his song, knowing that he hath wings."

Birds are often good forecasters of a change in seasons, by migration. When winter turns to spring, the buds of pussy-willows start to swell, sap flows, and flowering fruit trees in the towns burst with color, a Mountain Bluebird arrives to stand-watch and sing. Since music is the universal language of mankind (as suggested by the poet Longfellow), in Nevada we hear this supernal music, much of which is also heard around the world.

In the prelude to summer, the music of birds stimulates the sun (and also human beings) to rise earlier. We are awakened in the Truckee Meadows with the mating songs of Mourning doves and also California quail; we can be entertained all day- long hiking in Rancho San Raphael Park or strolling around Virginia Lake.

The early bird may catch the worm, but the second mouse gets the cheese.

Anonymous

House Finch

"You had to have a—"

Red-winged Blackbird swaying on a stem

Red-winged Blackbird announcing his territory

Certain Avian Serenaders

Noted references and guidebooks describe in detail the hundreds of birds native to Northern Nevada habitats. The following descriptions relate to only a few special songbirds of the area.

Blackbird, Brewer's,Red-winged and Yellow-headed

"Morning has broken, Like the first morning   Blackbird has spoken, Like the first bird."

From the hymn and poem
"Morning Has Broken"
with words by Eleanor Farjean

The Brewer's blackbird is completely black, except for some brown on females. It can be distinguished by its yellow eyes. The aggressive Red-winged blackbird also found in Northern Nevada and throughout the West has scarlet patches on the wing shoulders or epaulets. Its song consists of a gurgling three-note phrase. The vocalization is territorial and attracts females. The Yellow-headed Blackbird is a summer native of the marshlands. In addition to the yellow head, the male shows a white patch when it flies.

Bluebirds, Western and Mountain

Symbols of happiness, bluebirds are much too scarce for our tastes, and they are often driven away by more aggressive birds. Their declining numbers were often due to a loss of habitat. That has been countered by providing bird-houses. Bluebirds' presence can be encouraged by adding a new birdhouse with an entry hole one-and-a-half inches in diameter. The bluebird population is now increasing with the help of clubs, Boy Scout projects, and local Audubon chapter activities. Many golf courses have been decorated with houses for bluebirds.

Bluebirds have a soft gurgling song located in the upper range of the viola. The Western Bluebird lives in the lower elevations in Nevada. The Mountain Bluebird, the state-bird, lives at the higher elevations, around 6,000 feet. It is similar to the Western Bluebird, but without the rusty chest.

Chickadee, Mountain and Black-capped
A small, gray bird with black and white markings on its head, the Mountain Chickadee lives at high elevations in the summer and lowlands in the winter. In its major scale, the Mountain Chickadee often sings two fifth-notes above the tonic, followed by two major thirds.

Gray with a black cap, the Black-capped Chickadee has various short calls. "Its voice is "fee bee" "chicka dee dee"" [1]. It has a two-note whistle of an almost pure tone. Its singing has been the subject of research.

Dove, Mourning

"---I did mourn as a dove"

from Isaiah 38:14

The bird's name comes from the male's mournful song and haunting melodies. The dove is an emblem of grief; perhaps the lonely male is mourning for his mate. While not lacking in conviction, this Dove sings beautifully and somewhat dreamily, sort of a *dolce tranquillo,* describing a mood. In the first bit of warming in February, one hears the AAA-E-B. Their four to five note series of oohs or ooh-ooh-ooh reminds one of pigeons or owls but the song of the mourning dove is more plaintive. Mourning Doves give humans wake-up-calls early before daybreak, but they may be heard all day long. They sing in low pitches (alto or viola range)with overtones. It is a monotonous song, but the song is beautiful. Its soothing song often foretells a coming shower. Songs of Mourning Doves have many accurate musical descriptions such as *adagio, patetico, plaintive, lacrimoso, legato, andante, affannoso, con dolore, berceuse* and *sweet.*

Finches, Lesser and American (Goldfinch)

House Finches nest in hanging baskets or just about anywhere and entertain with warbling songs. Their music brings the beauty of spring and it continues into early fall. Their song is a long musical phrase.

Gold Finches and Purple Finches warble and chirp in a delightful series. The Rosy Finch is common in the mountains at bird-feeders and, like other finches, at nests in hanging flower baskets. Other finches often stay the winter in the mountains. They love bags of tiny seeds which they, and not jays, can hold onto with their feet.

Flicker, Northern

The Northern Flicker is a brown and black woodpecker. The male has a red mustache. They have a sound like "flickah", which the bird would be called in the state of Maine.

Flycatcher, Olive-sided

With the song,"qwik-hoo-hoo", these flycatchers inhabit the mountains of Northern Nevada in the summer and the low wetlands in the winter and they catch flies. They are dark gray with a white breast and neck, and perch in high conifers eating only insects with wings.

Grouse, Blue, Sage

The Blue Grouse is a small chicken-like gray bird with mating characteristics slightly resembling the Sage Grouse. It is found in the Sierra-Nevada range in Nevada. It produces low-pitched grunts.

   The Sage Grouse, like its cousin prairie chicken, has a different song. In Nevada, a flock of Sage Grouse gather in the spring at a particular location, and strut around, inflating their necks, and make booming sounds, like a percussion-like instrument.

Grouse, Famous

The Famous Grouse (*Spiritum Fermentum*) is almond colored with smooth characteristics and most often enjoyed along with the Wild Turkey in the evening lubricity. Male Snow-birds with tap-room noses are often observed in the vicinity.

Jay, Steller's and Western Scrub

The Steller's jay has a black head with a large black crest. It, like other Jays, is often seen chasing away and attacking small birds at bird-feeders. Jays are guilty of stealing nuts and other food laid out for squirrels; squirrels are also guilty of stealing food from bird feeders. I had to put a bird feeder on a wire between two trees to foil squirrels.

However, the sunflower seeds attracted a mother and baby bear. There is no solution.

The Steller's jay is a year-round resident of the mountains in Nevada. It builds nests of tiny sticks in trees and sometimes in other sheltered places around homes. The Steller's jay sings with a short series of whistles.

The Western Scrubjay is found in the lower elevations and is similar to a bluejay. It is blue and white with a black necklace. It is bold like the Steller's jay.

Junco, Darkeyed

A birdie with a yellow bill hopped upon the window sill,
Cocked his shining eye and said: "Ain't you 'shamed, you sleepy-head!"

by Robert Louis Stevenson

At Lake Tahoe, the juncos have been seen perching on the window sill. Their songs are a series of one-notes.

Kestrel, American
The American Kestrel is a small the smallest) falcon and has a high-pitched voice. Gray, brown and orange, it has a hooked bill and can be seen around the foot-hills, in the country, and in the city parks.

Kinglet, Ruby-crowned
It is a small bird, always flitting around; the male has a red patch on the forehead. Winter residents, they seem to depart for higher elevations or cooler weather in early summer

Larks, Western, (Lark) Bunting, Horned

You skylarks, circling free, sing loud your song!
Get through to worried hearts in melody
The message that the spirit must live strong
In spite of tyrants' might or will,-not die
We, too, may hope: so long as tyrants fight
Against the Truth we know that makes men free,-
For Heaven wills this truth may not be stilled.
Excerpts from poems and sonnets by Frank Kurz

> *If there were two birds sitting on a fence*
> *He would bet you which one would fly first.*

By Mark Twain in
"The Celebrated Jumping Frog of Calaveras County"

A harbinger of spring, the song of the Western Meadowlark, which may not even be a lark but a member of the blackbird family, is a favorite. Its music, a joie de vivre, is the most beautiful song. It resembles music of a piccolo or a flute. It is not a piece of abstract music, but repeated phrases, followed by a recapitulation coda.

After the cardinal, the meadowlark is the next most popular state bird. The meadowlark, with its light brown color, flash of bright yellow on its breast and white and black splashes, is usually seen on a fence or fence-post or on a bush. (The reason the meadowlark sits on the fence is to be able to jump into either field. Humans have copied that approach; however they often remain on the fence).

Meadowlarks' nests are on the ground making them an easy prey for snakes, foxes and skunks. They probably do not migrate.

The Western Meadowlark has an even more beautiful song than the Eastern Meadowlark, perhaps because there is more open-space for practice in the West, especially in Nevada.

The Western Meadowlark sings like the larks of Europe (previously plagiarized by Handel, Mozart, Aretrio, Cherubini, Schumann, Faure, and Gluck). Its song is quite different from that of a Mourning Dove, but it is equally beautiful and somewhat mournful. The song begins with a clear note rising in pitch then dropping, a perfect glissando.

The eastern and western species of the meadowlark are said to have dissimilar territorial songs but similar flight songs. Unfortunately, meadowlarks, like bobwhite quails, are declining in population.

The Lark-bunting, like its European cousin, has the most wonderful song, a classic repertoire.

Colors of the Horned Lark, like meadowlarks, are brown, yellow, white and black and their songs are a "tweet". When the Horned Lark sings, two small black horns appear. The Horned Lark sings in flight or at home in the fields of the University of Reno Farms or in desert ranges. Its song is a series of high-pitched chirps.

Magpie, Blackbilled
This bird mimics dogs, cats and people. It uses mud to build nests and is often seen around streams.

Merlin
The Merlin is a small hunter falcon like the American Kestral, with gray, brown yellow and white colors. The Merlin likes small birds. Its song is a series of "kwees".

Mockingbird, Northern

The Northern Mockingbird, which sings during the day and at night, especially during a full moon or under streetlights, mimics other birds. This bird may be singing while hiding in a tall shrub. Then it will fly away and return, or alight on a pole or wire. The long tail makes it easy to identify. It is gray with a black tail and has a white patch on each wing. The white splash becomes more noticeable when the bird takes wing. The mockingbird mimics the songs of other birds as well as other noises and songs. Mockingbirds sing their own compositions and those of other birds, frogs, pianos and other musical instruments. They even sing medleys. Mockingbirds have a great variety of sounds.

Nightingale

"That certain night, the night we met,
There was magic abroad in the air;
There were angels dining at the Ritz,
And the nightingales sang in Berkeley(pronounced Barkly) Square."

This is a very pretty melody by a British source. The Frank Sinatra recording has a bird-like trill in the instrumental background.

Nutcracker, Clark's

A(pinkish)gray bird with black patches on its wings and black and white tail-feathers, it lives near pine forests in the mountains. It comes to bird-feeders especially when snow is on the ground.

Nuthatch(White-breasted and red-breasted)

The male call is like "whee-whee-whee-whee" Other sounds are wip-wip, ank-ank, or a series of seven beeps.

When one is dozing in the hammock and sees a bird on a nearby tree going down the trunk headfirst, one can be assured it is a nuthatch and not a woodpecker. Gray and brown, with a white or red breast, the nuthatch walks both up and down the pine tree.

Oriole, Bullock's

The migratory Bullock's Oriole, like its similar cousin Baltimore Oriole, is distinctive by the hanging nest it makes. The male with the orange face has the stronger song than the yellow-headed female.

Quails, Northern Bobwhite, California and others

Deer walk upon the mountains, and the quail whistle about us their spontaneous cries

by Wallace Stevens-*Sunday Morning*

When we think of quails, the bobwhite, with its beautiful ascending line of two or three notes, comes to mind. When it sings, it slides into its top note. The name bobwhite may have originated from its beautiful song, a low "ah" followed by an ascending pitch resembling a whistle. The first note is a low(for birds) staccato followed by a slur rising less than an octave. That is called a "scotch snap", a short note followed by a long note. Sometimes the first note is a eighth-note followed by an eighth-note leading into the upward slur. The Bob White song is the lower range of songs of the bird kingdom. The bobwhite call is difficult to mimic by other birds, but it is easy to copy by a whistling human. It is native to Southern Idaho, common in the Mid-west, and found in California and Nevada. Sadly, today, the bobwhite is considered a declining species.

Years ago, after reading the book "That Quail, Robert", I ordered a clutch of Northern Bobwhite quail eggs and a small incubator and after the quails hatched, built an outdoor aviary, well fortified against raccoons. The quails lived outdoors, sang, and were easy to feed. They took dust-baths on the ground. After a while, one made a nest and laid a few eggs. When the last egg was laid, the mother started the process of sitting and tiny baby quails came and matured. I would whistle, admittedly with some appoggiatura (ornamental deviation from the true bobwhite song), and they would still answer. Even the neighbors liked them. After being frightened by raccoons, they were finally turned loose in a meadow.

The Northern Bobwhites, more common east of the Rockies but found throughout farmland in the West, enjoy grasslands, grain fields and hayfields with borders of trees, where they often gather. Coveys of Northern Bobwhites make a noisy exit when approached. Like other quails, bobwhites, when startled, panic and fly away in a mad rush.

Nevada has as many, if not more, varieties of quail as any other state. They include the Scaled Quail, the Northern Bobwhite, Gambel's quail, California quail, Valley or Southwestern Quail and the Mountain Quail. They feed on small grain, weed seeds, grass and insects. Quails are non-migrating birds.

The California quail extends its habitat to Suburbia. Outside the garage at home in Reno is a bushy weeping Pussy-willow, an ideal place for a nest of eggs. One morning, on August 1st, after being treated to a recording of *Ballet of the Unborn Chicks* from the symphony *Pictures at an Exhibition* by Mussorgsky, two adult California Quails and ten tiny fluffy, fuzzy newborns, marched out from under the big skirt of the bush and continued down the street as if they owned it. Perhaps they did. During mornings and afternoons, the California quails can be heard crowing on the hillsides with their songs projecting for blocks. The California quail has immigrated or has been smuggled into Nevada during the past two hundred years. Brown with white streaks and a black plume on its forehead, this quail's song is like cow(male) or chi-ca-go

Robin, American
A bird came down the walk;
He did not know I saw
He bit an angle-worm in halves
And ate the fellow raw.

Poem by Emily Dickinson

The American Robin is most pictured pulling an earthworm from the ground in the lawn and heralding the season of spring. Robins have gray backs and red breasts. They have a most-familiar song. The saying, "One robin does not make a Spring" is appropriate because robins are found year-round in most areas except in high mountains.

Robins leave a message for mankind(by Emily Dickinson): *If I can stop one heart from breaking, I shall not live in vain. If I can ease one life the aching, or cool one pain, or help one fainting robin unto his nest again, I shall not live in vain.*

Snow-birds

Snow-birds are migratory. They show up in the high Sierras or around Lake Tahoe about Memorial Day weekend and then flee south in the fall or no later than Boxing Day. They migrate to Arizona, Palm Desert, Florida or Texas. Unlike other birds, they usually migrate during daylight hours and stop for feeding, quenching thirst, and nesting in small villages along the way. Not all can sing.

Sparrow, Song

Beautiful music of these sparrows sometimes suggests an arpeggio, or part of a chord. They usually sing from thick shrubs, with bright short melodies. Their songs vary in flavor from locale to locale. Along with the American Robin, the Song Sparrow, with its whistle and trill, is a harbinger of spring. The Song Sparrow is a brownish bird with darker spots and a white underbody. The Song Sparrow is found in wetland shrubs and in thickets along the Truckee River. It is an optimistic bird that is always singing and cannot be left out of a list of musical birds.

Starling, European

The European Starling is a shiny black bird, whose vocalization includes mimicry. In the summer, the

European Starling has a yellow bill. It is often seen as a member of a large flock.

Thrasher, Sage
This gray bird, with white markings, long tail and a body slightly smaller than a robin, lives in the high meadows, where sagebrush dominates. A common location is in the Huffaker Hills in Reno.

Thrush, Hermit
Found in the hills and valleys of Northern Nevada, the Hermit Thrush has a most beautiful song with an occasional glissando and a Mozart trill.

Towhee, Spotted
From windows at Lake Tahoe, beautiful orange, brown, black and white birds can be seen at feeders. They are Spotted Towhees showing up in May. The male and female then started feeding together. They are also found along the Carson River. They move to warmer climates in the winter.

Warbler, Yellow-rumped
Affectionately known as butter-butt, it warbles, true to its name. It lives in low river valleys in the winter; then it moves to higher cooler elevations in the summer for nesting. Butter-butts are frequent visitors to the Truckee River. They have a yellow rump and yellow patch on each side near the wing. Their songs can be similar in rhythm to a samba.

Whipoorwill

The insect-eating Whipoorwill hides in bushes, trees and on the ground. Males sing for territorial reasons attracting the opposite sex. The name comes from its song heard before daybreak and at dusk.

Woodpecker, Downey

Seen around the Truckee and Carson rivers, the Downy Woodpecker has a white belly and white patches on top. It has a short beak with patches on top. An attractive sight, it can be seen in marshes, on cattails, or in trees or bushes

Wren, Marsh, House and Bewick's

Like its name suggests, the Marsh Wren, that practices polygamy, lives and nests in cattail marshes and other brush along streams and wetlands. Its song is more like chatter. It sounds like an auctioneer at a farm sale with rapid notes rolling off its beak.

The House wren sings a lot. This is a grayish-brown bird with a tail that is cocked.

Bewick's wrens can be found year-round along the brushy riverbanks and lakesides.

Western Sandpiper on a Reno street

California Condor

Water Birds of Lakes and Wetlands

*"And all I ask is a windy day with the white clouds flying, And
the flung spray and the blown spume,
and the sea-gulls crying."*

From *Sea-Fever*, by John Masefield

Generally speaking, birds of Nevada do not have to develop sea legs. There are exceptions: the California gulls and ospreys at Lake Tahoe, the Bald eagles seen at Spooner Lake, the swans at Swan Lake, the American White Pelicans at Pyramid Lake, the loons and various other locals and migrants in Carson Valley and the Lahontan Valley wetlands near Fallon. These lakes as well as Walker and Carson lakes are popular stops for migrating water birds along the Pacific Fly-way.

Duck, Wood

The Wood Duck, like the Mallard, is a most beautiful water bird, with splashes of red, green, purple and tan. It roosts and nests high up in trees, but the young birds quickly find their way to water for food and play. The Wood Duck can be seen on the edges of streams, ponds and lakes.

Eagle, Bald

*"But those who wait on the Lord
Shall renew their strength;
They shall mount up with wings like eagles,
They shall run and not be weary,
They shall walk and not faint."* Isaiah 40:31

We will call the raptor Bald Eagle a water bird only because it is often seen on a tree, post or pier-post looking for fish. Winning over the turkey, whose song is a "gobble", it was made the national symbol of freedom in 1782; the Bald Eagle has held a special status in the United States since its early formation.

The Bald Eagle was becoming rare in the 1970s, but now its population is steadily increasing, and it is no longer considered endangered.

The Bald Eagle can have a life span of 70 years. Bald Eagles are diurnal and are usually seen around Lake Tahoe, Spooner Lake and other Northern Nevada lakes as well as in pastures during the winter months. They have a wing span of up to seven feet or more, and are said to reach a speed of up to 200 miles per hour when diving for food, which can be fish, rabbits, rodents or carrion. Like the osprey, the Bald Eagle builds a large nest of sticks usually near the top of a tall tree and close to water. The Bald Eagle has a snow white or piebald head and neck giving it the appearance and name "Bald" Eagle. It is sometimes called the American Eagle, bird of freedom, as well as other names.

The naturalist John Burroughs wrote these vivid words: *"He draws great lines across the sky; he sees the forest like a carpet beneath him; he sees the hills and valleys as folds and wrinkles in a many-colored tapestry; he sees the river as a silver belt connecting remote horizons".*

Goose, Canada

There swims no goose so gray, but soon or late she finds
some honest gander for her mate.

(Pope)

The Canada goose is listed under water birds only because it is often found on a golf course near a water hazard. Some comments were made in a previous chapter so there is no use in boiling fiddleheads twice.

The country of Canada is frequently disparaged for various things it has no control over: cold winds, the Canadian clipper, Chinook winds, Canada thistle and even the Canada goose. Some lakes are protected by fake swans to discourage the Canada goose. Its lifespan can be as much as 20 years and it is know to be faithful to its mate. When chilly weather arrives up north, it is common to see more flocks of Canadian geese appear on a golf course at a lake shore. Then they make honking noises in the transition to becoming airborne. When one talks, others chime in until all are talking at once. They are most vocal in flight.

Gulls, California

A quiet picnic on the eastern shore of Lake Tahoe, or a sail under a tall mast, can suddenly be interrupted, when one tosses away a piece of bread. All of a sudden, a flock of beautiful, crying white birds sail in, one or two gulls bingeing like a duck on June-bugs. The flock then circles and glides and provides entertainment for a while. Perhaps a few lone gulls will remain and occasionally cry out for the treat that they missed. Then they leave to follow O'Malley's fishing boat.

The gull sound is a sound pleasantly reminding one of being near the water. California Gulls often migrate hundreds of miles inland to breed, perhaps at Mono Lake, and return to the coast for the winter.

The Ring-billed Gull is found in abundance at Virginia Lake in Reno. In January, 2008, a rare dark gull was seen at Virginia Lake. It is presumed to be the first appearance in North America of a Lesser Black-back Gull, a native of Asia.

Kildeer
The Kildeer is a member of the plover family, a shorebird with long legs and a song "kil-deer" It is brown, orange and white and moves to a warmer climate in winter.

Loon, Common
It is a large migrating loon found around some lakes, such as Walker Lake and Pyramid Lake. It dives for fish and can stay under water for a long time. The Common Loon has a hauntingly beautiful song, not unlike the sound of an oboe, often starting and ending on the same pitch with a middle note a major fourth higher in between, then followed by the same sequence transposed a major second higher. Loons are seen floating on the water with their long bills parallel to the surface.

Osprey
The Osprey is a large gray-brown fish-eating bird, often seen at the top of a dead tree on the Western side of Lake Tahoe. Ospreys build large nests on dead trees and on poles. They migrate to tropical areas in the winter. They

are knowledgeable of aeronautics, turning its fish catch forward to reduce wind friction in flight. Their song is a chirp starting with an *accidental* above the main note.

Rails

Two Rails heard and seen around marshlands are the Virginia Rail and the Sora. Each has a distinctive voice like a grunt or a "kwee". Pond owners often are plagued with duckweed. Soras eat duckweed.

Shoveler, Northern

A group of nearly one-hundred shovelers were seen recently at Virginia Lake in Reno. They were in a close-knit assembly moving clockwise, then counter-clockwise, making a whirlpool to stir up food. The colorful brown, green, white and orange water birds with large bills are fascinating. They sometimes can be seen in a tight circle among a wide collection of Gulls, Mergansers, Canada Geese and Pied-billed Grebes.

Swan, Tundra

The Tundra Swan is a large white bird. Hundreds of these birds migrate from near the Arctic Circle to Swan Lake (with its convenient boardwalk),north of Reno. Their song is a soft honk.

Swan, Black

Not all swans are white; black swans were discovered in Australia(but never in Nevada) in the 1600's. It was such an unpredictable event that the term "black swan" has been used and books written to describe the phenomena of high-impact unpredicted and unexpected events.

MINI, MIDI, MAXI — I WANT TO SEE MY GAL'S FEATHERS

"mini, midi, maxi—"

The Birds and the Bees

"Birds do it, Bees do it,
Even educated fleas do it,
Let's do it, Let's fall in love."

From a Gershwin musical

One similarity between birds and bees is that both bees and some small birds provide plant pollination. The rest of this section is not necessarily fit for young minds.

Birds' love is based on the Greek word *eros*. *Filial* love also exists, but *agape* love is non-existent in birds. Quoting Andrew Berger, "The breeding season is the focal point of a bird's life". Mating time can be stressful for birds. The male (occasionally even a monogamous one) may not be able to eat or sleep and its tiny brain may be in overload during this romantic interlude while he sings and makes his courtship display. Some birds are somewhat indiscreet during mating season.

Spring is around the corner, but "Baby, it's cold outside"; why not climb into the nest together? It takes two to tango. Birds, some monogamous and others polygamous, may start a romance with the *pas de deux,* a dance announcing their intentions. Some males attract mates with their colors, their beautiful colored plumage and unctuous personality; others become troubadours; some have not a scintilla of those characteristics. In other words, some look good, while others attract by their personality and the sounds they make. Females seem to like the best songs. Males from their perch will first sing to males, persistently announcing their territories. Then they turn their attention to the females, not altogether different from tenors with enthusiastic singing in a classic opera. Melodious birds attract mates. Is mating a thing of enjoyment, or is it just the method of maintaining the species?

Well, it must arrive as a result of hormones when the female arrives on the scene.

Some birds are known for fidelity, but the male Red-winged blackbird is most polygamous with up to ten or more females occupying his territory and hearing his familiar song. Generally speaking, "birds of a feather flock together".

Courtship leads to nest-building, feeding the female and copulation, similar to the human series of events.

"You never find out what I'm to wear-"

Yellow-headed Blackbird

The Art of Listening

I only ask for time and tranquility

- Hector Berlioz

After silence, that which comes nearest to expressing the inexpressible is music.

From *"Music at Night"* by Aldous Huxley

But we, how shall we turn to little things,
And listen to the birds, and winds and streams.

A poem *"Lament"* by Wilfrid Wilson Gibson

Are we afraid of silence? Silence is necessary for good listening. While music in early civilizations was limited to solo singing and percussion, it evolved to cathedral choirs and putting words to music in the fields and on the streets and in bistros. Today, many people, mostly young, spend a portion of each day listening to music on the Walkman, Zune or I-pod.

Birds still sing. How often do we really listen to birds singing? A walk along the Truckee River can be an opportunity to listen to a symphony in the Pioneer Center Opera House, Nightingale Hall on the UNR campus hearing Jennifer Day, clarinetist, mastering Messiaen's *Abyss of the Birds* in Nightingale Hall or in Oxbow(Nature Study Area) enjoying a sandwich and listening to birds. Birds' music is especially rich along riverine thick brush and everywhere else during the mating season in spring or early summer. When bird-singing is first noticed, the song can be amplified by cupping hands behind the ears.

A bird's pitch seems to rise if the bird is moving closer or drop when moving away from the listener. This is called the Doppler (Fizeau) effect. This phenomenon is also experienced listening to a fire or police siren or train whistle.

Where did the popular Rhythm and Blues originate? Perhaps it grew out of music from the song sparrow and mourning dove. The birds' warbling, where notes run together or slide, has been copied by famous country singers such as Hank Williams and George Jones.

In this locale, the Truckee, Carson, and Walker Rivers, Spooner Lake, Pyramid Lake, Swan Lake and further afar, the Red Rock Canyon Natural Conservation Area and Desert National Wildlife Range are likely habitats for listening to birds' songs.

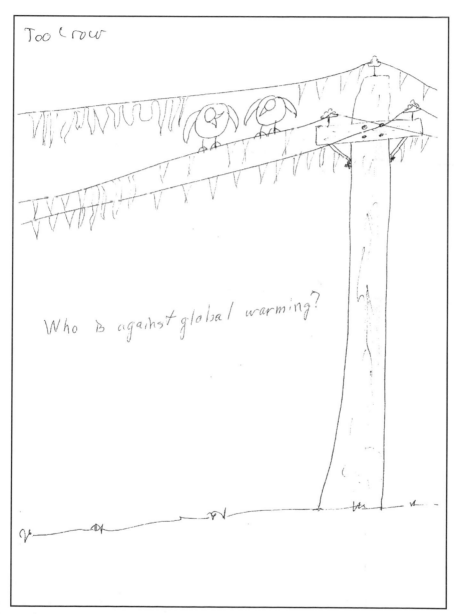

"Who is against global warming"

Finale

These are the days when birds come back,
A very few, a bird or two,
To take a backward look.

Poem by Emily Dickinson

As autumn arrives in Nevada, migrating birds arrive from the North seeking longer days in meadows, lakes and marshes. Some continue south and others stay. Birds are no longer singing to attract mates but Canada geese continue to make noise.

Swainson's hawks are winging to Argentina. California quail are staying. Mergansers gather at Taylor Creek to feed on dying fish returning to their birthplace. Robins head south for the winter.

Indian summer is a perfect time for birding at marshes and along the Carson and Truckee rivers.

The bird you thought was yours-took wing and flew away

-Bizet's *Carmen*

Autumn came and the nights became cool and longer; valleys became a pale or bright yellow mix of cottonwoods and aspens. The trees are ready to shed their colorful leaves. The days grow short. Fur of the squirrels is thickening. Peavine Mountain is white. Many birdwatchers have put away the binoculars, spotting scope and camera.

Excepting melodies from Song Sparrows, the birds' songs are few.

The perfect disc of the sacred moon
Through still blue heaven serenely swims,
And the lone bird's liquid music brims
The peace of the night with a perfect tune.

Poem by John Masefield

Summer for thee grant I may be
When summer days are flown
Thy music still when Whippoorwill
And Oriole are done.

Poem by Emily Dickinson

The Canada geese are here
They slide across the new ice
They are at home in cities and towns
From V-format they soar
To meadows and the shore
To march along with low honking sounds.

On a mid-winter morn
Some Moffitt geese are circling
The fairway traps are buried in snow
They have no place to land
Lo-there's a strip of sand
They glide to a winter home below.

Poem by George Griffith

Canada geese ignoring the sign---

List of Illustrations and Photographs

Index (of birds)

Bibliography

1. Rappole, John H. <u>Birds of the Southwest</u>. College Station, Texas: Texas A&M University Press, 2000
2. Grout, Donald J. <u>A History of Western Music</u>. New York: W.W. Norton &Company, 1973
3. <u>Nature Conservancy Magazine.</u> Spring 2003
4. <u>Reference Data For Radio Engineers.</u> New York: Howard W. Sams and Co.(ITT), 1968
5. Beletsky, Les. <u>Bird Songs (Featuring Audio from the Cornell Lab of Ornithology)</u>. San Francisco, California: Chronicle Books, 2006
6. MacKay, Barry Kent. <u>Bird Sounds</u>. Mechanicsburg, Pennsylvania: Stackpole Books, 2001
7. Flugum, Charles T. <u>Birding From a Tractor Seat</u>. Ed. Merlin Flugum, St. Paul, Minnesota, 1973
8. Vanner, Michael. <u>The Encyclopedia of North American Birds</u>. Bath, United Kingdom: Paragon Publishing, 2003
9. Stanger, Margaret J. <u>That Quail, Robert.</u> Philadelphia and New York: J. B. Lippincott and Company, 1966
10. Lemmon, Robert S. <u>All About Birds.</u> New York: Random House, 1955
11. Van Tyne, Josselyn and Andrew J. Berger. <u>Fundamentals of Ornithology</u> New York: John Wiley and Sons,Inc., 1959
12. Mathews, F. Schuyler. <u>Field Book of Wild Birds and Their Music</u>. Honolulu, Hawai'i: University Press of the Pacific, 2004
13. Levitin, Daniel J. <u>This is Your Brain on Music</u>. New York: Penguin Group, Inc. 2006

14. Stokes, Donald & Lillian. <u>Field Guide to Birds(Western Edition)</u>. Boston, New York, London: Little, Brown and Company, 1996
15. Terris, John K. <u>Songbirds In Your Garden</u>. New York: Thomas Y. Crowell Company, 1968
16. Macdougall-Shackelton, Scott A.;Weisman, R.; Ratcliffe, L. Relative <u>Pitch and the Song of Black-capped Chicadees</u>
17. <u>A Birding Guide to Reno and Beyond</u>, Lahontan Audubon Society, Editors Karen L. Kish, Alan Gubanich, Ph.D.
18. Forshaw, Joseph; Howell, Steve; Lindsey, Terence; Stallcup, Rich; <u>Birding </u>. San Francisco: Fog City Press, 2007
19. Berger, Andrew J. <u>Bird Study</u>. New York, London: John Wiley and Sons, 1961
20. Peterson, Roger Tory. <u>Field Guide to Western Birds</u>. Boston: Houghton Mifflin, 1990